FIREMAN JIM

FIREMAN JIM

by Roger Bester

CROWN PUBLISHERS, INC.
NEW YORK

Also by Roger Bester
Guess What?

Manufactured in the United States of America
Published simultaneously in Canada by General Publishing
Company Limited
10 9 8 7 6 5 4 3 2 1

The text of this book is set in 14 point Lubalin Graph Book.
The illustrations are black-and-white photographs.

Library of Congress Cataloging in Publication Data
Bester, Roger.
    Fireman Jim.
    Summary: Text and photos describe the job of a fireman and
observe his twenty-four hour shift in Manhattan as he goes to a fire
drill and battles a real blaze.
    1. Fire fighters—Juvenile literature.   2. Manhattan
(New York, N.Y.)—Fires and fire prevention—Juvenile literature.
3. Marron, Jim.   [1. Fire fighters.
2. Fire extinction]   I. Title.
TH9418.B47   1981   363.3'78   81-9694
ISBN 0-517-54290-0   AACR2

To fireman Jim Marron, Ladder 3,
and the New York City Fire Department

JIM'S DAY

New York City fireman Jim Marron lives in Babylon, Long Island. It is 6:15 A.M. as he leaves his house to go to work. He arrives at the firehouse on East 13th Street in Manhattan. Instead of his usual 8-hour day shift, Jim will be working what firemen call a 24. He will be on duty from 9:00 A.M. Sunday to 9:00 A.M. the next day.

JIM'S JOB

Jim drives a ladder-rescue truck called Ladder 3. Six men ride the truck—five firemen including Jim, and the captain. Jim is responsible for the truck.

Ladder 3 is part of Battalion 6 in lower Manhattan. The battalion has a car for the chief, two ladder trucks, and three fire engines. The engines carry the hoses.

Fire alarms are received by the central office and relayed by computer to the firehouse closest to the fire. When all of Battalion 6 is called to an alarm, Ladders 3 and 9; Engines 5, 14, and 33; and the chief and his aide go. If the alarm is a 10/18 (radio code for one engine and one ladder, no additional help required), the chief sends the others back.

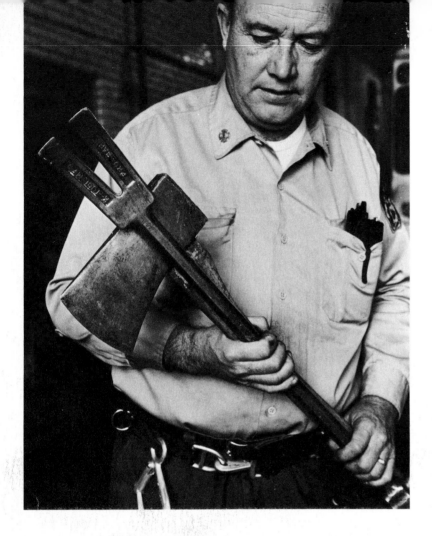

Jim checks his ax and crowbar and
the saw that cuts through anything.
Fire does not wait, so fire-fighting
equipment must always be ready
and in working order.

Oxygen cylinders and masks prevent the
firemen from being overcome by fumes.
All the firemen hang their fire-fighting
clothes and radios close to where they ride
on the truck. Jim's hang by the driver's door.

FIRE DRILL

It is Sunday morning, fire-drill day. Fire drills are for firemen to practice working together and to learn new techniques. At a fire there is no time for mistakes.

Jim puts on his boots, hat, radio, and coat and drives Ladder 3 to a parking lot.

At fires Jim is responsible for manning the ladder,
which can reach up to 100 feet. It is used for climbing
onto buildings and rooftops.

After the drill the firemen go grocery shopping. They buy food for their lunch at the local supermarket. The captain and all the men go. Each man has his radio turned on so he will know of an emergency call even when he is busy buying spaghetti, tomato sauce, soup, bread, and coffee.

When the firemen get back to the firehouse, the alarm sounds. In less than two minutes Ladder 3 and its crew are on their way. Fortunately the fire is not serious because the fire department was called on time.

JIM'S NIGHT

It is 6:00 P.M. Jim will be on watch duty for the next three hours. Jim is responsible for the computer and the incoming calls. Most calls are routine and not all are fires.

Jack is cooking tonight's dinner of lamb chops, Brussels sprouts, and pecan pie. After dinner Jim lies on his bed upstairs, while the others watch television and relax.

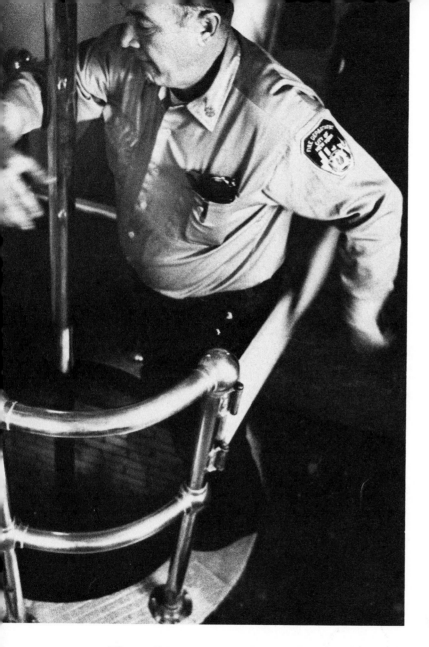

The silence is broken by the sound of the alarm. Jim slides down the brass pole to the truck and joins the others as they put on their fire-fighting clothes.

FIRE This time the fire is serious. The top floor of a house on East 19th Street is on fire. When Ladder 3 arrives at the building, the tenants are already safely on the street.

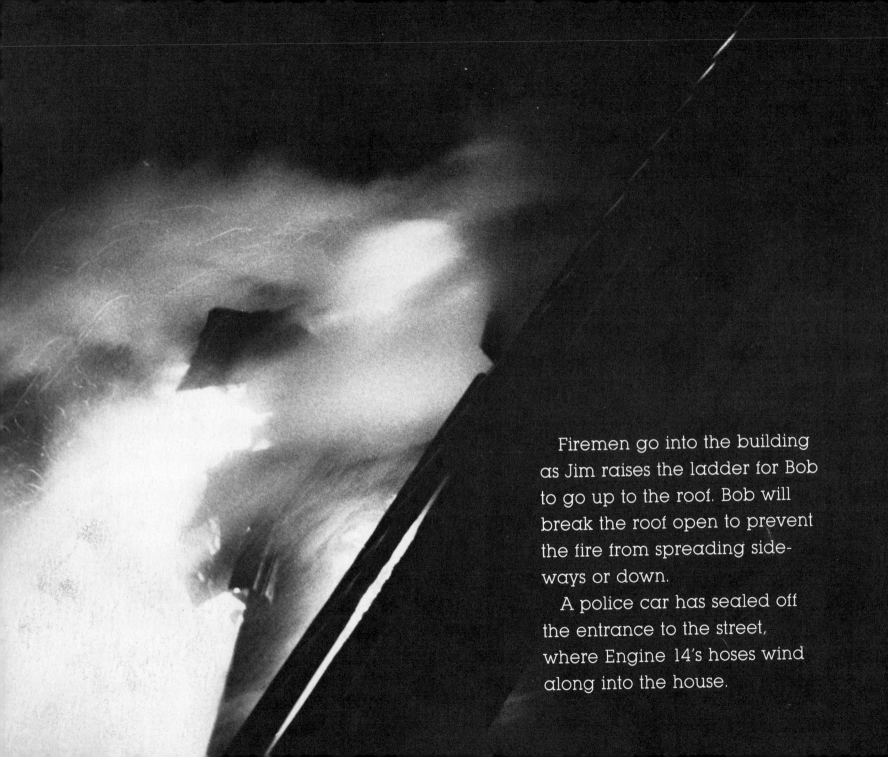

Firemen go into the building as Jim raises the ladder for Bob to go up to the roof. Bob will break the roof open to prevent the fire from spreading sideways or down.

A police car has sealed off the entrance to the street, where Engine 14's hoses wind along into the house.

After a last look outside, Jim puts on his oxygen cylinder and mask to protect himself against the smoke. He enters the building to the sound of shattering glass as the firemen break windows to let the flames out.

Inside, the heat is intense. It is a dangerous job, but the flames are now under control. Where there was fire there will soon only be smoke.

AFTER
THE FIRE

Jack and Jim are tired and tense, so they rest a while. They have just finished ripping away burned window sashes, doorframes, and floorboards to make sure no fire remains hidden.

Before they leave, Jim calls the central office by radio:
"Ladder 3 is 10/8. K." The code 10/8 means that Ladder 3
is once more available for service. K means the end of a
message.

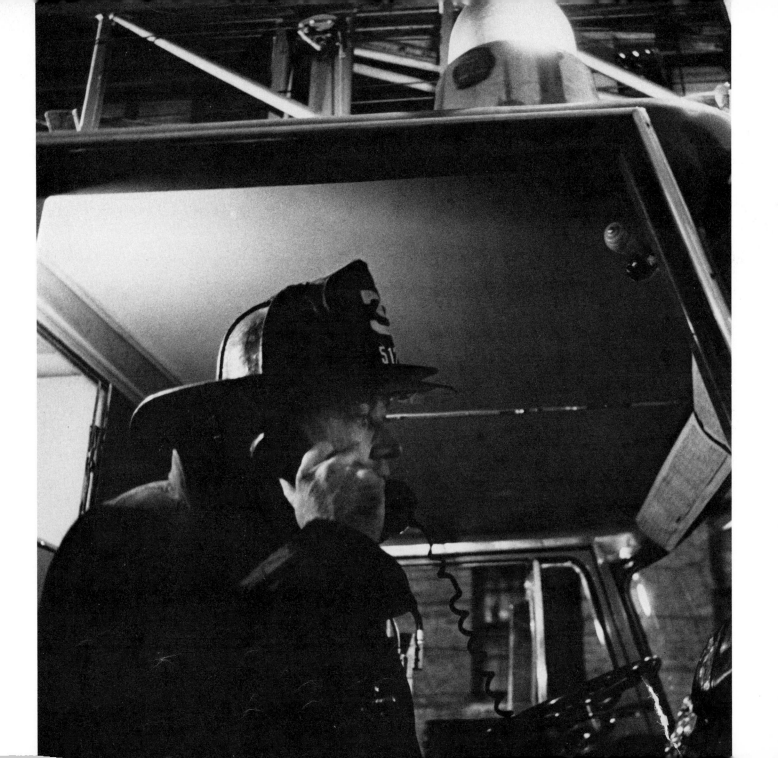

It is 4:00 A.M. when Ladder 3 returns to quarters.

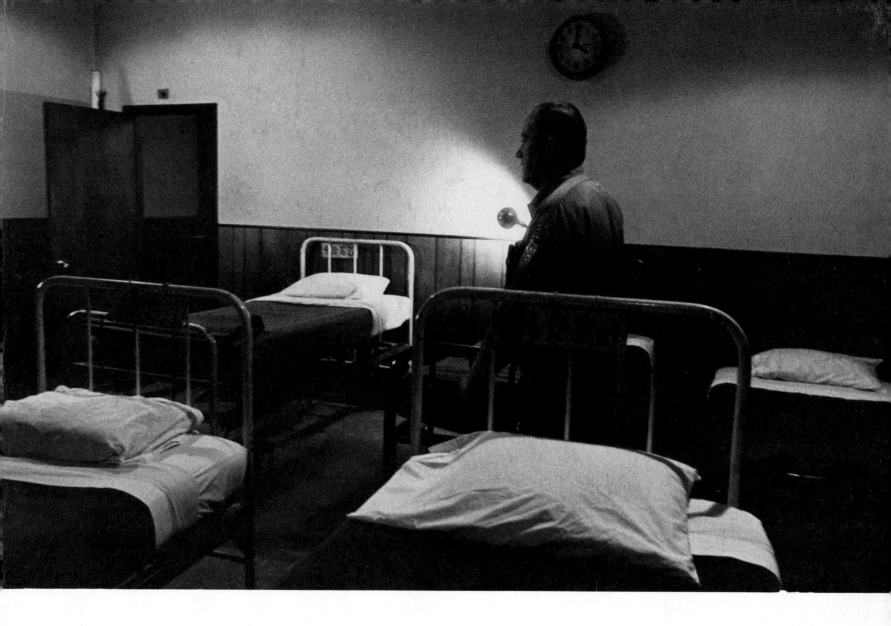

Jim goes up to the dormitory to sleep. That night there are no more alarms. He sleeps until morning.

It is 11:30 A.M. when Jim arrives home.